Meta-Fore!

(and other golf-related injuries)

By MJ Monty

Some names and identifying details have been changed to protect the privacy of individuals. This is a work of fiction. Names, characters, businesses, places, events and incidents are either the products of the author's imagination or used

in a fictitious manner. Any resemblance to actual

persons, living or dead, or actual events is purely coincidental.

I have tried to recreate events, locales and conversations from my memories of them. In order to maintain their anonymity in some instances I have changed the names of individuals and places. I may also have changed some identifying characteristics and details such as physical properties, occupations and places of residence.

Any political speech is protected by the U.S. constitution.

Table of Content

To allow madness is an escape.

To drink is to hide from truth.

To remain ignorant is impossible if

one already knows.

The lazy man fears work.

The manic dreads rest.

The simple are happy in their way.

The wise are aware and free, choosing discipline.

Journaling the world for a day,

a life, in a day,

an hour, in a moment.

Dramatic nonsense of feeling,

the illusion of length and meaning.

The shared gravity of humanity and

our vanity to disregard it

to escape.

A word to a sentence

A day to a week

A thought for an idea to build a philosophy

to escape.

Beings competing with other beings:

to be.

Rush hour, work week, precious moments

we codify in routine, ritual, rite, and holiday.

Still holding and

held to earth by

gravitational grips and

habitational gripes.

Our prophets and salesmen cry

"Escape!"

And we cannot tell the difference. ~

This collection of thoughts, bits of humor, political speech, and personal agony is the writing after my second publication, "Public Private Places." Before PPP, **Vox Noir A Radio Drama**, was published in 2016 (676 pages).

Meta-Fore! (and other golf related injuries) is the beginning of my departure from self. The Table of Contents is a means by which you can skip over the boring parts and get to some fun stuff. Mixed in is a collection of poems titled Perils Apart.

Meanwhile, I am changing. My thinking is changing. Let me explain:

I believe I am about to think differently, therefore, to be different. I might live new, different thoughts, leaving the circuit, the shape, the course, the current, for the shapeless unknown, the whisper of what I've heard over the years but never learned.

The clutter of life, the crowding and padding of real persons: the clothing we put on, the coverings, the barriers we accumulate for ourselves until we feel nothing or no longer hear the now muted Spirit. Clogged ears, and corrupted hearts.

Then the awareness awakes. We hunger and thirst for peace within. We find helplessness in how to leave self. Where is the teacher for this? Where is the power? I have already been captured. I have already been purchased. I do not belong to my "self" but to God. My "leaving" has already been granted permission and passage.

I will not leave Him. I cannot leave Him. So, what of my departure? Who or what am I leaving behind, setting aside---escaping? Treacherous ground and treacherous air are just outside "me." I, like all others, have found my comfort and misery in what I know: what is mine. But I am being called out of the comfort, out of the current. I am a fish summoned to the air, a man asked to walk under the sea.

My forehead rests

against the bedroom

garage wall. Legs are

spread by a pillow.

An award-winning foreign film

cobbles language and woodwinds helpless,

but I am primary to the coolness of

my flattened skin.

The mistake is to mistake

the moment for meaning,

as so often I do

to make a life.

I add hour to hour

in a day

to make the end

a grand resolution.

The muscles in our feet

in our limbs, mark the walk,

the week,

the turn of the century,

the lady's hat "when."

When art and artist stop speaking,

to sing.

And the musician stops directing,

to dance.

Then the world will have put on its final coat.

The light darkness of the happy mask,

the metal paint and the soft shot.

I see love withdrawing

without a bow. I see and feel

the strings and wires played

by the spider.

Distraction is only a note.

Deception, just one instrument.

Destruction, a working title.

True holy men are unseen.

True madmen are quiet.

The "real" I sense, is without

sense.

Need starves for want of will.

The greater systems that need us

for blood, walk in strides, the world,

to move in coercion.

The sons and daughters who were

born, not made, do not escape because

they were never here, not a word, an hour,

a moment in this world, never this life.

They started eternity early. ~

There is a place here,

with the block threatening the blank.

I laugh.

What constraints?

With writers: the past

With writers: the future, they

have not live yet? Erroneously we

romance facts and pain.

I am free but as much as they?

I fight for the morning word

probably as much as they did.

So, to coffee, and the possibility

of leaving earth.

The rush to word,

the struggle to pull the balloon down

by the dandling thought.

And then we have it!

And it changes, and we become

an anchor for an idea.~

The dimensions of new thinking: Phrases such as "Broaden one's horizons" "wide spectrum of thought." Solomon had an "enlarged capacity to understand." There is "depth of understanding" in contrast to "shallow" thinking. I am persuaded to believe that if I do "think anew," I will be leaving my smaller room for a larger one.

I do wonder if in my attempt to embrace "new thought" with my old senses, I will deafen and blind revelation and instantly relegate it to my small room instead of allowing it to take me out of my understanding. This reminds me of the concept of insecurity.

"A fool is right in his own eyes." He insists on his familiar living quarters and will not trade up or trade out of his comfort. I am confronted thus with my first fear: that I cannot escape my own gravity. The teacher is willing to teach but is the student willing to receive, to abandon "what he knows" (pride, security, identity: real or imagined) to step into the previously unknown (new knowledge)?

It's why I didn't want to read books when I was writing. I did not want to be influenced by "others." I was not sure of my own identity, my own thoughts, or voice. I didn't want to assume someone else's thinking and therefore identity.

I joined a religious cult when I was 17 years old. I was young and unfinished. My ability to think and decide were disrupted and manipulated. I came out four years later, damaged and aimless. After 30 years, I have gotten most of my marbles back. I have struggled over the years to recover my "self." What I found out is that the self I finally isolated and labeled as me was insecure, immature, corrupted.

The job ahead, as I see it, is two-fold. I need to identify and replace false teaching and thinking about God. I also need to face what is true about me, the good and the evil, and then find truth that will bring about real transformation. It is cleansing the inside of the cup.

Is the new thought or thinking just the initial or old thinking? God has been speaking from the beginning. This is not a new commandment but an old commandment "that you follow love." "New" is new to me not God. "Greatness" is greatness to me and other human beings, not God. My anxiety about time and being late to God's will is my worry, not God's because He walks around and over time. The "new" thinking can only come from the one who was and who is and who is to come, the I AM. Otherwise, I am left with my guesses about Him and His will. I am helpless with the tools I've picked up to fix myself. ~

Emotions

and God,

God's emotions,

my emotions in the image of God's, and

my fallen emotions in the image of corrupted flesh.

There is confusion.

God's anger doesn't look like mine.

His reasons for wrath aren't mine.

God's anger, hatred, indignation, silence, sorrow,

all the negatives--- are not human.

But we humans, in His image,

imagine Him as one of us.

And we are wrong. ~

In the booth, about the field,

educated spectators comment

on the action of beings below.

The announcer, the perched nest, temp-controlled,

padded for the think-speakers,

the talkers, the interpreters of the game.

But we need them, don't we?

We need someone watching the same

event to tell us what we are seeing. We need

someone in the room with more at the ready:

resources, graphics, and vocabulary.

Radio contact used to be the only necessity

for the man out in the field to hear the

play-by-play of the hometown team in

an away game.

Now everything is home.

Everywhere is here. We can

see everything, hear everything,

care about everything. Even pretense

of pretend phobias and scaffolded dramas

have a channel.

Could we bear silence,

see blindly nature

and what it tells us?

Can we live without cameras,

without recording, without

the men in the top box, parroting stats,

slo-mo's, and worship?

What happiness,

without the middle

between us

in HD.~

If you could manage off-self and

To-others, you would live longer.

If you could get the "you" out of

everything and make everyone not

"you" but them, then your life would be

richer. I dare you to think about me.

care about my life, just today. It wouldn't

take much. You would lose control. You

would find relief away from yourself and

I would find you.~

The romance of waiting for a train.

All the hard work is done, riding the damn thing.

Those waiting are tubbed, combed, and checking their

pieces.

Horse manure is in the off.

Cattleman and farmers keep

their weather vane hygiene schedules.

Maybe the soaps and perfumes

were made stronger then, to

last more than a day.~

<u>Mistake at An Interview (5)</u>

"I'm a very private person. I'm not really

comfortable with questions. I thought

maybe we could just talk about superficial

things for a while." ~

Barak the Great, First King of America

Part of my duty as an American citizen is to be political aware, engaged, to be constantly vigilant with my fellow citizens so that our elected officials will experience our consent and their accountability. A problem has arisen from our vigilance. We pay too much attention and create and nurture the narcissists who thrive on our captive senses.

A honest question that is rarely answered truthfully is why someone wants to be the President of the United States? It would be helpful to know what reasons the first five presidents had for seeking the office. My guess is that their motives were more honorable than those who have held office for the last

100 years, with a few exceptions. To the honorable, such a query would have been offensive, I suppose.

George Washington could have been president until his dying day but he served two terms and retired. The American government in many respects was a contrastive answer to the English monarchy and its tyranny. Washington modeled the moral behavior of a servant leader which we rarely see today in our politicians.

We now have term limits for our presidents because unlike Washington, the more recent occupants of the office don't want to leave the stage. More recently we have been treated to the lingering presence of one Barak Hussein Obama, 44th President of the United States who seems so insecure about his legacy, his place in history, that he took up residence in Washington D.C., shortly after leaving office.

And only after a little over one-hundred days of the new administration, Mr. Obama officially reappeared in public and is involved in some sort of quasi-political leadership, last seen/heard inserting himself into the Jimmy Kimmel healthcare monologue with a tweet of support for Kimmel and a little chirp of promotion for himself and his abysmal healthcare law.

I was under the impression that unwritten proper decorum for former living presidents who respect the office and the will of the people was to retire with quiet dignity for at least a year or so, allowing the current Commander-In-Chief to govern without the former's glorious residue confusing the governed.

Surveying the presidents of the 20th and 21st centuries, I find Mr. Obama particularly troublesome as some of his loyalists within the current administration answer and act, not to President Trump, but for him.

President Bush (41) and President Bush (43) left office and stayed away long enough for us to appreciate them. President Carter went on to build houses for Habitats for Humanity. President Clinton has been less gracious in his self-imposed, semi-absence but President Obama I fear will never go away.

He will make speeches and meddle in elections foreign and domestic. And as long as his loyal surrogates are in our government, we will never entirely enjoy his exit from public life. It is our punishment I suppose for electing a man who genuinely believes that "it is all about him." After all, "He is the one he's been waiting for."

Therefore I have crafted a solution that is tailor-made for the 44th "former" president and his devotees.

Perhaps by constitutional amendment or some congressional action we can anoint Barak Hussein Obama the first king of America.

I see this as a great pressure release and relief for all Americans including Mr. Obama. His desire is to be in charge with all eyes on him, accepting the adoration of grateful citizens that are alive and able to witness his life lived before them. Many are content with the eight years afforded Mr. Obama and wish, as I do, that he would go back to where he came from and leave us all alone. So to make everyone happy, let us create a limited monarchy for him.

Let those who wish Obama's continued rule be compelled by him to donate a portion of their take-home pay to fund his house or castle. Let one of the cable/satellite companies grant him his own royal channel to which his followers can subscribe on a pay-per view basis. King Barak can be covered by any media source but his speeches, public appearances, or any image of him must be confined to the royal channel. All broadcast outlets must turn over their interviews, coverage of any future royal births, christenings, worship services, etc., to the royal channel so that most of the country can watch TV safely without any surprise visits from the king.

I believe that, with the money collected by the Royal Treasurer, King Barak could live quite well and feel very important to his subjects. If he wishes to make his wife Queen, then an additional financial edict can be issued to the people who voted for him. His political power and influence would be as consequential as a British Monarch's on Parliament, that is to say, hardly impactful.

My memory of my brief study of the monarchies in history informs me that kings were anointed or they performed some feat of renown to be declared or designated royal. This ancient criteria makes it difficult for me to qualify Obama for contemporary majesty. Let's work with what we have.

The first King of America has to be born. He does not need a record of accomplishment. He must have a strong sense of entitlement. These qualifications could also be applied to other politicians who find it difficult leaving the limelight.

I mean to say, what future president is going to call former President Obama for advice or counsel about anything? What has he done for the last eight years that would commend him to any leader quest for wisdom? Has he shown any expertise in foreign policy or domestic policy? He was really good at looking the part.

He was symbolic, a figurehead, a dynamic placeholder, everything we could ever want in a king. He could read well.

Based on the amount of money the King's subjects contribute to the royal treasury, The Obamas could live very well for the rest of their lives and American taxpayers would be relieved of the burden of supporting them, hearing them, or seeing them.

I think if my idea works, it could be extended to the Clintons. King Barak, by decree, could make Bill a Duke or an Earl. If Michelle does not want to be Queen, King Barak could offer the throne to Hillary. We could confine them all to the royal channel, the royal castle or RV, depending on funds, all out of sight and mind the general public.

Some of us believed that when his two terms were up, Obama would go off into history and stay there. We did not vote for Hillary, hoping she would get the hint, that we really didn't want her to lead the country or be seen or heard from ever again.

For the sake of the health of our nation, we citizens need to concentrate on the reality of our American Constitutional republic. Those who wish to check in with their king can do so at their own expense. If my proposal is enacted by Congress then perhaps we

can all get back to holding our president accountable:
our one, current president.~

<u>Writing the Woe</u>

Some want it so,

so it goes. And some want

but not the way it was,

rather the wish they dreamed when

a movie, the playhouse screened.

The liars want power, the story is

theirs and they tell it to lead,

to the leading man before he is even born.

The people under the floors and in the walls,

shift the foundation, desperate to get a word

to the builders who put them there.

Hard to have a state dinner with

mumblers behind the plaster, whisperers

dusting the ceiling. We toast the pretender

while he sits on the bones of children, eases

back on the weaves of flesh. The wine is red

and thick. Laughter is skull chatter. Who will

write the true beginning if it excludes them from

greatness? Who of the godless can serve without

homage or worship?

Philosophers cannot be heard over

the drama of illusion.

We trade truth for the look

and the like. If we think ourselves creators

 then worship ourselves, we.

The delusion is self-inflicted in a pill or a drink.

We prefer sleep because we live heavy.

We can escape while still breathing.

Why did I take this hammer?

Why did I understand it this way?

Why did I look for loop holes?

Why?

Because I'm still here. ~

   A honeybee landed on the buckle of my open
journal. I tried to take a picture of it with my phone
which only works in the reverse since I laundered it. The

bee left before I could turn my camera around and guess where the shutter button was on the opposite-side touch screen. I could interpret this at least two ways. I could get a new phone or I could learn to live in life instead of trying to capture it.

But isn't the artist, the middle-man, the in-betweener? It is the glorious partnership of God and man, the revealer revealing revelation to the being He made for his pleasure: to speak, to construct, to express to everyone else. Impression and Inspiration are expressed out to impress, imprint, impart. We speak, sing, dance, paint, play, and breath, truth here. Eternity is different. We are one, there. ~

Insecurity: the acuteness of our dependent nature. We are born fallen. We come into the world dependent. We need others. Insecurity is developed by deprivation of love.

If our parents intentionally, unintentionally, or through absence, fail to provide the necessary securities of love, we become insecure and will seek power, love, strength, control, perfection, collections, masteries, whatever will secure our insecure core. ~

Sorrow: to see the future

and have no way or means to change it.

A prophet knows going in, that

he is a reporter, that he speaks not to change

hearts or influence men.

He speaks not his own words. And he is

not exempt from the warning nor protected

from sin. He also is accountable for the words

he utters.

God does not choose His prophets among

the sinless. It is not the vessel's righteousness

but His mercy and love. ~

In a foreign world

the air is visible to hearts.

A pod of young humans

collect to rebel which

reminds me, why I left,

why I fled south.

They did not notice

my speech but climbed

over my body for the next high, for

the next feel.

I am confined to a room full of criminals

and I cannot speak.

A class of young animals with flared noses.

I sat down with my younger self and tried to

reason with him. All that was missing

was the glitter, the wind sparkle, the great

distracting shape I called "thinking."

I see what's ahead of him.

No eye contact, no sound. He uses his

keyboard like a xylophone. I used my IBM

Selectric to shoot down planes.

Time killers, time wasters, time delayers

and delusion. But the punch line is later

when time takes its toll, and he's

empty-pocketing the corner for change

from the quiet ones who paid attention

in class.

I cannot preach or pastor.

I cannot control the unwilling.

I cannot prescribe and jam down

the cure.

How, for 3 years, did our Lord

teach a people that would one day

kill him?

The rebels are not true to

their stated cause. They are

not heroes in the fire.

They are gluttonous brats

who laugh their way to starvation,

fat fools who wander into old age

never knowing their own life

before death. ~

I noticed the change and

unchanging, daily. Old age

isn't sneaking up on me.

Being a narcissist and fully

aware at all times of the

symptoms of self, I run

system checks with every

beat and blink.

But there is also our internal design

and perception of time. We recall

instantly the memories of toddlers

toddling and then juxtapose this

with the man or woman in front of

us and reach the wrong conclusion,

that years haven't built the being. Armed

with the same mechanisms of perception, I

review my aches and pains and project the

effects of age into the future. Years go by like

months. Twenty years doesn't seem like a generation.

What I care about now filters my perceptions. Pain

and comfort now corral decisions and a course that

will finally bring me the infantile movements of old age.

I used to wonder how old people got old, examining their choices of food and clothes, and the things they talk about. The process is happening now. The choices are offered now while our durability and the longevity of our bodies bear witness to time.

Our bodies are like automobiles. They come in a variety of styles and colors but all the essentials are the same. How we treat our bodies when we learn to use them will determine how well we get around in our last years. Those who abuse their bodies put unnatural mileage on their frames. I look at those who drank, smoked, and drugged in their youth and see early death and premature feebleness.

If we live for the moment, for the present, we will later reap the result of foolishness, lust, and appetite. ~

We stop from our lives

to look at things. And we

stop from things to see ourselves

in their context. We put them there, all

that's around us. We collect to mark

childhood. We gather the army

or savior to make permanent

the moments when we felt safe

or loved. In our wisdom we let

loose what we pretended was

love or meaning. We are wise and

unhappy with what is left. Only

a fool delights in the childish. It

is the fate of the wise to be sad.

They understand the origin of things.

They know the end of the song.

The loneliness of the wise, one

could sell by the cup on a corner.

Lovely is the silence he enjoys and

the light foot traffic of a foolish world

to his door. He has place settings furry

with dust. His clock can be heard in the hall.

Still a lark or a house-martin may search at his sill.

A raven wouldn't dare perch, now that he's so poor.

Careless the cleaning woman, and forsooth, the letter
box.

We women know the heads must be over the wall
for the sake of the city. It is not likely the gentleman will
call.

I bless the coming of the new age, when

harrows and furrows will cease their wrinkle.

Tea is drunk all over the world, save

this sitting room, where a walrus

towers and tusks, because I was lonely

and he failed to grip. ~

A teachable moment

is not

a moment that can be taught.

More accurately: a teaching moment,

       a moment in which to teach.

In truth if someone says, "This is a teachable moment"

one cannot argue. For it is at that precise moment that

one can correct the misuse of language.

"You" are teaching at the moment you isolate

the present to instruct another being.

So, would someone please come up with a

pithier way of saying what I just said before I impale

myself on the next white forest unihorn? That's right,

damn it, unihorn. And change February to Febuary.

It sounds better and kids can pronounce it. And

get rid of daylight savings time. It's not necessary

anymore and it screws people up. Stick to the one

where the sun is already up in the morning.

The government should not be so prevalent.

Everyone wants to be wanted, but needing

to be needed is perverted. ~

Tiny realities distract fantasy.

I tear down most everything until

what is left

is true.

Wise man waits out the fool

by walking away.

He'll not find a pause in play

to this endless escape.

Beware the offered drama,

to drug you like a drink, to

distract you from the dull drums

you dance to daily.

Chasing the world for a piece of it.

Treading the mill for each crumb.

I wake up to grind and ground all purpose.

It cannot be that

outside skin and walls,

someone else is living and

waiting for me. ~

The world wants your eyes,

your ears. If you turn away then

it turns to bring you back to

see and believe against God,

against your soul.

Wisdom brings sadness, vexation,

and grief because it tells us how

pointless life here is,

how it ends, that there is pain,

that there is delusion, and

hopelessness. That by God

we survive, through suffering,

that beauty varies and true beauty

is on a continuum.

Life is dimensioned and methodical.

With ropes and routines we capture

pieces of it for our existence, ever

searching for what is eluded to

with lies, from those who never

knew joy. ~

<u>To a Place</u>

Come to

going to

Arriving at

no grand entrance

to a place

of confrontation.

The common law of

mid-life is to find

a corner or a pond,

a border stream or

a childhood haunt

to sit down for

inventory and assessment.

A book or a map cannot

help you to this place.

Advice can only start you

on your way there. Questions,

you carry on the footpath. Doubt

and hope take turns on

the fringes. You know where

but know not what and that

is why you've come.

"I cannot shed my familiar clothes

nor can I leave the wheel without help.

Why then do I come to no one and expect

a listening ear?" Because no one is listening,

has always been since your first word and before.

He made what you have come to and

he knows why you are here. Always present

in the present around and over eternity. So

sit down or kneel before know one and be known

by Him. It will make all the difference to your

"now." ~

I remain volatile against clocks

and workers watching screens

for the thinking they used to do.

Wires tell us: plug-ins, pixels, cartoons, and

signs we cannot find in the natural life.

If it is,

it

isn't

it.

That's why children are innocent

before we corrupt them

with toys.

We all need a song, a smile,

a thumb drive, a scream saver.

I am impatient with anyone

in line, in front of me, unless

they entertain, loosen my anger

with some organic apology for our

mutual pain. ~

<u>Mistake At the Interview (6)</u>

"You remind me of my last boss.

He was really serious too."~

<u>Blow Up the Mountains</u>

As technology improves, so does our ability to gather and disseminate information. We listen or look is still our choice although the encroachment on our free-will is becoming almost impossible to prevent or deflect. Whether it is the entertainer who wants our eyes and ears or the politician, the portals for our senses are open around the clock. In order to get away, we need to turn off the windows and run to the nearest nature. We will return eventually and face the consequences of "missing something."

What bothers me is the quality of the information that is presented. When exactly did the phrase "news *and* commentary" come on the screen and page and become acceptable journalism? I thought news was reporting the facts. Who cares what someone's opinion is unless the person can bring a better understanding of the facts. Political talk has become sports talk, with "expert" commentators who cannot predict the outcome or the winner of anything.

This whole "global warming" now "climate change" fiasco is a colossal example of scientists with a political/social agenda mixing with foul politicians who will say and do anything to gain power and control of the population. Albert Gore Jr. is not a scientist. He is a politician. He surrounded himself with data and politically compromised climatologists to further his power and financial well-being.

Rather than take on Mr. Gore's hypocrisy and/or his silly notion of "carbon credits" whereby a person can pay for his own pollution, I propose a little task or test for the former Vice-president. I will go so far as to offer suggestions for solutions to this little project. Instead of trying to avert a global catastrophe or a national crisis, why not focus your attention, Mr. Gore, on one region, one part of one state in our union, one city: Los Angeles, California.

Can you, Mr. Gore, reduce or eliminate the pollution in the San Fernando Valley? Fog plus smoke (exhaust) makes smog. It's man-made pollution, your greatest enemy. Whether we humans are changing our climate or are even able to do so is still not settled no matter how severe your persecution is of those who dispute your "findings."

Let's start small. Now, how do we eliminate the smog from L.A.? I am not a scientist but neither are you, Mr. Gore, so let's brainstorm. I was told or read somewhere that the reason why the smog in the valley does not dissipate is because the surrounding mountains and ocean act as a kind of bowl and the air pressure above the area functions much like a lid or ceiling. Cars by the millions expel exhaust and contribute daily to the air quality of the valley. The pollution, having nowhere to go, remains on top and next to the people living and working Los Angeles.

I propose two possible remedies. The first idea is a bit drastic and the second is a more moderate approach. I suggest we blow up the mountains. I am not sure which mountains should go. I would have to consult geologists and people who understand wind currents and circuits. I am partial to eliminating the mountain range that contains the Grapewine. The few people who live and work there can be compensated for their loss of business and/or property and be relocated.

Once mankind is cleared from the heights, we send in the bombers. My guess is the explosives would have to be conventional and not nuclear. We need something like a Bunker Buster, something that could dig down and disperse rock and dirt effectively. The military could estimate how many earth-shifting munitions we would need to get the job done. Dump trucks and haulers would work around the clock for years removing the soil which would create "shovel-ready" jobs.

Of course, problems would arise and if you go with this first plan then you will have to address north/south travel up and down on I-5, and commerce dependent on that route. Just a side idea--- build a truck highway parallel to the 99 and the 5. Trucks could drive up to 100 mph and the other highways could be just for cars.

If blowing up an entire mountain range seems a bit too extreme then perhaps a modified version of plan A. Why not bomb a crack right down the middle of the mountains. The width of the crack will depend on what is needed to create a vacuum. The smog needs to escape and we can't take the lid off (air pressure) so why not crack the bowl. Find the strategic location and bunker-bust down to sea level. This will only work if the air pressure to the north or east is less severe than the atmospheric pressure above the majority of the population in the valley.

If the smog needs help going through the crack or fissure, we could build a tremendously large wind farm either on the inside of the bowl or on the outside or both: one farm blowing the smog out or to the north and the other sucking it through to the other side. When I say wind farm, I do not mean those turbines one already sees on landscapes where wind already exists. I mean large electric fans.   Since Mr. Gore is enthusiastic about electric cars and wind farms, why not combined the two to pull and push the smog out of the affected areas. Problem solved.

If Mr. Gore adopts my plan then he could name the finished product the Albert Gore Mountains. Might I suggest taking a page from those who named the Grand Tetons, French for "the Great Breasts." The people in the

Los Angeles area could rename the new topography the El Burro Grande Mountains. The people north of the range would simply refer to them as The Big Ass Mountains. ~

Finding a way to walk with the crowd.

One can only go as fast as whoever's

in front. Hard to shepherd and sheep

simultaneously. The pasture is fense-less

and I need sides. Religion is secure, faith is

free-fall in every direction.

Ritual and method build lifeless

stone upon stone.

Shapeless airs indwell

small God houses but

the Rock is alive.

The Spirit is

not earthbound and those escaping

the world hitch a ride and are mocked

for their levitation. ~

This is not Wysteria again.

She was finally accepting of earth

and its immoderate topography.

The fence just in front of the gravel,

just in front of the sliding glass door.

We are sentries posted before the gray

onslaught of another storm. The knot

holes in the wood drew the attention

of the philosopher behind his pen.

Knots are nots: holes that used to hold

plugs which, reverse engineer the

planks back into trunks, were the anchor ports

to branches and limbs which no longer exist.

But the holes are here, emptiness defined by what's

around them.

To a child, a world

through a wood window.

To a man, what was.

A reminder of what was. ~

"America is the only place

where people who don't know

what they are talking about can

say whatever the hell they want."
> (MJ Monty ...after watching the
>
> 2017 Academy Awards.) ~

Surrounded by the familiar,

how can we resist the

gravitational comfort?

To step out into the air on

a notion. To accept the invitation

not delivered by a smile, but in

tones of indifference, even disdain.

The rainy day man attempts sunlight

while the blaze of color

moods down to

overcasts

under the blankets.

The dry fount heaves and hurls dirt

before the thirst of a woman.

Stare out the window for sun and

think of night at noon. Counter the

irrefutable. Use what fists you can

make with your made-up mind.

It is not against settled truth that

we contend, but against the beliefs we

were taught to be true.~

Can we become friends so late in life

when so much has already been cast

and set? Yes, because love and truth

are eternal. Only we can fail

      if,

        only we.

How grand our lives, how large our

presence in a small room. If we go out

to creation to the Creator,

we find our insignificance

and His great love. ~

I began a word

to make a sentence

out of habit, thinking

you

here.

But empty chairs and bed,

voiceless tabletops and

indifferent weather

counter my thought of

you here.

I found a stage and

set the players in parts.

I casted you in the lead,

this time, and

me to follow.

No one came to watch.

I can't pay the actors enough

to stay and you were always

in your dressing room,

deciding. ~

I would write my death today if not for the rain
and the little hope it brings by its short life. I would call
for a hearse, hail a cart, flag down a wheel-barrow, but
for the comedy I feel, sitting on a wet cushion beside the
wind chimes. Anger is in the off and will remain so as
long as I keep smoking.

I am confronted by sex and it demands a report, a
reckoning, a settling of accounts. I face, yet again, a
beggar for your affections.

I won't die today.

I was promised not to.

Not death but

life in passion.

Cruel bars of a soft box,

allow me to see

not embrace what is

distant near. But to say

only one comes to assail me

is deluded hope. They all come,

all the number of my regiment:

the administrator and the dish boy,

the salesman, the smoker, the child thief, the boyhood liar. They all come for a say.

I laugh at the truth that they have always been, were always speaking.

But today, because of my defeat, my resignation to self-interpreted truths, they rally for the podium, line up to have a go. They know I won't die today. Vanity preserves an unwithering face and the freedom of an ignorant dream.

The rain will stop and

leave only cold beauty,

an outline I can trace

without you.

Send not the mourners today.

Save the hushed voices for the sun.

For then I'll be gone. ~

WhereWhyWhat?

Recently there was thrust upon the country a kind of protest of sorts called the National Womanless Day: a day without women, so to speak. The idea, I think, was that those of female-kind would withdraw from their work and/or domestic responsibilities, and boycott the various goods and services offered to one and all in order to awaken the "patriarchy" to the value and worth of womankind.

While the turn out for this event was scant, the opinions expressed about the minimal mass absence were overflowing. I first thought of the mangled message these women had collaged for some unspecific audience. I reacted by paralleling in thought this "protest" with the Black Lives Matters movement.

It struck me the same way. The BLM message and call to action was predicated on a misinterpretation of a police shooting in Ferguson, Missouri.

As far as I could make out, the target of BLM's grievances was the local police department and then was expanded to include white police officers who were members of larger city police departments.

Finally, the message settled on all white people hating all black people in America. President Obama did not help at all with mending or healing when he invited members of the BLM movement to the White House and validated their hodge-podge kitchen-sink approach to civil disobedience. His previous comments about law enforcement also contributed to the strength of the BLM cause and our confusion.

After I ran through my own analysis of the National Woman-Free holiday, how their acts of sequestration were in many ways inconveniencing the very women they purported to represent, I considered the protest concept in a general sense. I asked myself the catch-all, all-encompassing question: why?

Why do we humans roll up the sleeves and clear the throat, or in the case of the fairer of the sex, rearrange outer and under garments before placing before the populace some wrong that needs righting?

Was there ever a time in history when vocal protest was efficacious in the matter of social change? It seems to me that those who were willing to raise the rifle or posture a pistol were the true rebels who, in a word, were revolting. They were committed to revolution which meant a strong commitment to truth against an injustice to the point of death.

The trouble with the modern-day protester is that he or she has only a cursory glance at a hint of truth while swallowing and caring around a political distortion concocted by some emotional college professor or wrong-headed politician.

What, I ask myself, every time I am forced to witness these political spectacles, is where is the truth in the complaint and is it a reasonable position to support.

One premise that I refuse to entertain at any price is this notion that women are supposed to be considered and accepted by the bushel, by the case, or in gross. Having married a woman successfully and having continued for some time now in the matrimonial state, I have never been under the impression that I was yoked to a gaggle rather than a soul in the singular.

It seems to me that the only people who view people in groups are those steeped in political, philosophical, or religious ideologies. It stands to reason that a system that derives its power from a voting electorate would wish that that voting electorate would be, could be, or should be corralled into manageable pods and kinds. The philosophical and religious have their own forms of crowd control but that's another piece.

Jolly difficult for a shepherd to get all the sheep going his preferred way if Sheep A is murmuring to Sheep B that the shepherd is talking through his hat when it comes to the subject of greener pastures.

I do think the "women's movement" and BLM are derivatives. They hail from tragic injustices done one-hundred, two-hundred, and four-hundred years ago. The contradictions they face are current realities and the evidence of progress. We in the audience scratch our heads and half-heartedly lean in to hear the grievances because they sound hollow when set against what is actually true NOW!

These women who are driven to display their worth by not displaying themselves may understand to some degree that their complaint is based on a true tragedy from years past. The Black Lives Matter attendees clumsily use slavery but more recently the treatment of black people in the South as a crude contemporary support beam for their platform. But it fails to hold those of us who live in the 21st century.

At the heart of it all, and it is impossible to discern accurately "all hearts" without being guilty of "grouping" people. There are universal truths. This is one of the things I have been looking at recently: local and universal truths, and how to apply each. Why would I protest? Why would I join a group and carry a sign? And would signs and chanting be enough? Then there is telling the truth about myself to myself before taking to the streets.

I am a selfish American brat in my mid 50's. I must conclude that there exists the truly and genuinely aggrieved plaintiffs who are surrounded by purposeless wasters who find energy for their aimless lives by creating a mob. True believers are exploited by the political entities who are willing to surf over their bodies to power.

The quality of the protest and the protester depends on the ratio of Truth vs. Self-Centeredness. The current crop of protesters strike me as brats who grew up into older, uglier, political versions of themselves.

The result of a society that saturates its senses on entertainments and stimulants is apathy toward the meaningful and worship of the meaningless. Contrived existences are coined into "reality" shows. Those who tell the truth are called liars because it is more exciting and entertaining than "thinking" and then obeying what is true. We want to know how our leaders will make us feel and not where they are taking us. I used to wonder how the antichrist could deceive the whole world. I don't wonder anymore. ~

I have become more acquainted

with my own urine

in these late years. I've

discovered the meaning of

old inventions, what inspired

their making. I want things

and people to make sense,

to mean more, because for so long

nothing has. Insanity is bliss to one

who is fully given to it. Those who

pretend madness are tethered to others
perceptions.

I judge myself as melancholy,

as not pretending but knowing

the marks and signs

of the blessed.

I should not be so old, this young.

Life happens to the ordinary li-ver, who

wore out his eyes and thoughts on meaning.

I never learned to hear the randomness

of rain and understand its nonsense.

We will not see ourselves the same as before,

but we will be common to the ridiculous,

plain to the wall climbers.

I keep from going mad by

running ahead of boredom.

I make meaning even from a shoe,

or in the stucco's ridges and ravines.

I fine animation in the inanimate.

Imagination is allowed for the sound mind.

I just need to remember

not to believe

what I dream. ~

Wanderers about the cities and

parking lots,

The lunch rooms and

parks,

Animals scavenge for hearts.

Love in a can or wrapped in foil.

Bootlace drag through mud-tracked lines.

The chatter at the snack stand, the

nonsense dance to wordless tunes.

Harmless deaths report true to

the lovers who miss the signs,

wandering around for second looks.

The stomach-in—chest-out promenade for

the judges who shout "single" to the parade.

Desperate animals for affection, ravenous,

senseless for touch, past the age

of desirable, past the prime or peak,

the other side of the mountain with

its back to the sun. The search turns

inward and fasts on the scraps.

The plans of the mariner,

the babble of the explorer:

the lady believes, if he takes

her along.

The conqueror of the schoolyard

is the best in his year. Life is glorious

in the moment.

But give it time.

The revelation exalts

those who live on the

valley floor. ~

Today, I didn't think once about death.

I've been awake for hours.

In the morning commute with

no working radio. A

heightened sense of age.

Reminders and pangs,

if any, are as loud as

the crackling aches of

my diesel in idle

on the 805, waiting

for the break

in the slow.

Spreading the budget

across the windshield:

gas, bills, and food.

My figuring gets me north,

for Christmas, if I borrow again.

Return, the heroic failure.

All hail the crate pulling in

from the 5.

I don't think about death

Not today. ~

What comes to mind,

to ear

is Brom or Brohm.

The sound of drums

with brown finality.

The Brohm is not final but

beating a wide skin. It

recedes when the lunchroom

chatterbox cuts through the

bass with clattering facts about

the excitement of her mundane mop.

It was the same yesterday.

Brohm, brohm-

chitchitchitchitchit with variations

and modulations for the hearers

of which I am reluctantly

a friend.

Brohm, Brohm—

chitchitchitchitchit.

My grapefruit, peeled and pulled

apart is my next desperate grab

at hearing the beat of my Brohm,

which belongs in such weather.

The pink-white fruit and its juice down

the wrong pipe signals a break in tempo.

The erratic recovery is more interesting than the

choir collected around the soloist.

Soon the gathered will gather around

to when I was a listener. The vacuum fills as

the shore cannot stay dry. I take in the

smaller pieces so as not to drown and

risk the possibility that someone will

notice and include me.~

You know you've made the coffee too strong, if,

after a cup, you believe in yourself. If after two cups,

you dream of being driven to work, while driving.

And when the thermos is gone, you give yourself

a promotion and work is beneath you.

The morning wears on and the coffee

wears off. The grandeur which immersed you

drains down. You're hopeless till lunch, where the

bottle or the can awaits to assist you back to self-
worship.

It is in the evening when all your dreams fade and fail.

And so bourbon will mourn till morn.

Today can be erased by tomorrow's today.

And you wonder why nothing changes? ~

<u>Shake Johnson</u>

*This piece of writing was in the first edition of Vox Noir, A
Radio Drama, set in Dallas TX, 1995:*

Mark wondered how Phil was. Chet was fired
after Mark's death. KNGT changed its format. Mark

couldn't tell if Phil was behind anything or even in the city. He sat down in front of a café at a sidewalk table and dialed in Limbaugh while he nursed an iced mocha.

Mark didn't have ear phones and so everyone within several feet of his table could hear the host of the EIB network at work on 'another excursion into broadcast excellence.' Mark wasn't sure if he was annoying anyone but, because of his present mood, he didn't care.

Limbaugh was saying something about Farrakan and his Million-Man March when a man sitting close enough to Mark's table piped up.

"You a dittohead?"

Mark turned around.

"Oh, well, yeah. You mean a Limbaugh fan? Yes, I listen. I wouldn't say I'm a dittohead."

Mark was sensitive about labels or being grouped into anything even if he agreed with it.

"Whatchu think about Farrakan?"

Mark felt like he was being corralled, assessed, and vetted.

"My name's Mark."

"Shake Johnson."

"I think Farrakan is smart, elegant, and wrong."

"You got that right. Million Man March, damn! What's the play? I don't think he got his number. You see him on the tube?"

"Yeah. I don't understand his thing. He sounds like he is trying to help black people but then when he was asked about the 'Jews' comments or 'white folks' he doesn't quite answer directly."

"Cokie, Sam, and George done opened up on the huck and he did his hat and cane routine. I listen to Limbaugh and read and I figured some things out. I have a view. You want to hear it?"

Mark didn't want to say no but he was secretly trying to listen to the radio and Shake at the same time and it wasn't working. He turned the radio down and tried to concentrate on the human being in front of him.

'What is your view? I'm all ears."

"Damn, Mark, you don't have to broadcast it. Damn, you sound like you should be on the radio, and you don't even need a microphone. Know what I'm sayin?"

Mark laughed. "Sorry, I can't hear how loud I speak."

"My view is this. I mean, my answer to all this racism shit. You want my answer; the thing that'll fix the damn problem?"

"Yes" Mark said quietly.

"Shut the fuck up."

"What?"

"No, not you. I mean that's the solution to all this crap about racism and white supremacy and whatever bullshit their shoveling: 'shut the fuck up.' Do you know what I'm sayin?"

"What, like, everyone stop talking about it, and then the problem will go away?"

"Exactly. Starve the monster and all his teeth will fall out. Why is there racism in this country, Mark? You tell me."

"Well, we had slavery here and white people treated black people terribly."

"Mark, you ever own a black man?"

"No."

"Yo daddy own a slave?"

"No, my dad was a migrant farmer growing up: dirt poor, picking fruit, up and down California with his family. My dad is of Mexican descent. I traced my family back to New Mexico, when it was a territory, into Meoqui, Chihuachua, Mexico. I traced back to my great, great, great, great grandfather. He didn't know his parents so the search back ended in 1718: no conoce parentes."

Shake waited for Mark to finish. He didn't think a simple question called for a run-down of family history which took him so far away from his original point.

"So, yo daddy worked in the field. He didn't own anyone who worked in the field?

"No. He went on to the Naval Academy and finished his career as the Chief of Civil Engineers. He went from dirt poor to working in the Pentagon. He's on a commission right now, appointed by President Clinton."

"You a damn chattabox, aren't ya. That's fine, that's fine. In a way yo daddy proves my point but let me get back to it. Neitha you nor yo daddy nor all y'all picking fruit in New Mexico or wherever the hell Meoqui is, owned slaves, right?

"Right."

"But you say we got racism today because of slavery. Why do you think that? Answer me that. Why you go to slavery when I fus mentioned racism. I tell you why---because some people won't shut the fuck up.

Now listen ta me. Slavery been gone for 130 years. Who is still talking bout it? Some black folks. Why they still talking bout it? There's your big question. You can answer that one. Why they still talkin' bout it, man?"

Mark was still trying to take in the likes of Shake Johnson.

"You can't answer cuz you a white man talkin' to a black man bout slavery in America. I tell you why some black folks still thumpin' the box. Cuz they want money. They got a message. They got an idea. They sellin.

Somewhere it says, 'As a man thinks, so is he.' That's the Bible or some fortune cookie. You know why some black folks act the way they do? Cuz they been taught what to think about they selves, about what white folks did."

"But that's history. Slavery actually happened."

"Oh, we gonna do this again? You own a slave? Yo daddy own a slave?

Why we talkin' about it now? Folks been taught that whites beat, whipped, and killed they ancestors. Shit, what about today? What about me and you living right now. Folks crying about slavery today are either out of they damn minds or they want money; money they didn't earn. No white man shot my son dead fo years ago. The asshole was a Mexican.

Now, should I hate all the brown people, huh? You half Mexican. Should I hate you? Should I blame you? You gonna give me money because you related to the Mexican who shot my son?"

Mark clicked off the radio.

"I'm sorry about your son."

Shake was quiet. He had his own thinking and Mark seemed to be the first or only person he found who would listen to him.

"So, back to my point. How do we fix this? I'll tell you. Jesse Jackson and Sharpton and Farrakan should shut the fuck up. All the history books and history teachers should just shut the fuck up about slavery. I ain't sayin' we never teach it. I'm saying we all should take the next 20 years not talkin' about race, color, or any damn slavery.

You know why the government been on education so damn hard? I mean, yo democrats and yo republicans been trying to control the schools in America foreva. You know why? Because if they control what the kids in school learn, then they can get control of the grown-up man and woman.

Martin Luther King Jr. talked about a color blind society. Damn right! How about a color deaf society or a shut-the-fuck-up society? You tell a black child from the ground up that whitey is the problem, whitey gonna keep you down, whitey owned yo great, great, grand daddy, whatchu gonna get?

Every election the damn newscasters talk about the woman vote and the black vote like none of us are individuals, like we all in some kind of tribe or herd. Fuck that. Hey newscasters, shut the fuck up!"

"But the Constitution, I mean, free speech. You can't tell people what they can and cannot say. I mean, you can but you can't stop people from talking."

"No, I can't. No I can't. But if you want to fix the problem and the damn 'black leaders' don't, then everybody got to stop talkin' about it."

"I agree with you."

"Let me ask you something, Mark. When I fus got yo attention, was you 'fraid?"

"A little. But that's not because you're black. I get defensive when any stranger talks to me. I don't trust anyone."

"Fair enough. I was going to say that if you was afraid, it was because you don't know me. That's the other side of the coin. We fear what we don't know, but that's another cup of coffee.

We stop talking about racism, it dies. We stop looking at it, it dies. You ask me, the real slave owners today are the damn black leaders, keeping us chained to the past. I got a job, I got family. I'm living. Someone wants to mistreat me, that's their problem.

Plenty of shit in this world. Damn Irish got crapped on when they fus got here. Italians, Germans, and the Japanese caught shit during World War II in this country. Indians really got the raw end. Don't get me started on the Jews. My answer: forgive and forget and I mean forget it all.

Chewing on my son's death ain't goin bring him back. Giving the guy who shot him the 'lectric chair ain't gonna make me happy. Messed up world, so shit is bound to happen. I ain't sayin don't never talk about history. I'm saying we should take a generation off or two and then come back when people's got perspective.

Black folks don't got no perspective and they ain't taught none: runnin' around angry at whitey when they got bigger problems than whitey right in they own damn yard."

"I hear what you're saying but what about slavery. No, I didn't own any slaves. But what would you tell the person who says the government of the United States made a promise to the black people of that time, something like 40 acres and a mule. Doesn't the government need to do something to make it right?"

"So you're askin' the U.S. gov'ment to give today's black man 40 acres and mule?" Shake smiled. "Nah, I know what you mean. U.S. gov'ment gotta pay money to black people. Nah, that's not gonna happen. First of all, all the slaves they owe money to are dead. Those folks they whipped and killed are gone. The only folks who have a real beef are dead.

Black folks today are taught they are just like the folks who got whipped. No damn perspective. So, 130 years later, some black folks want money from the gov'ment because they ancestors were slaves. You gonna have some kind of gov'ment agency trying to find out who came from slaves and give them money? Let me ask you something. You pay social security, right?"

"Yeah"

"Okay. U.S. gov'ment takes yo money and they gonna give it back to ya when yer old. What if they can't? What if they won't? You gonna fight the gov'ment? U.S. government makes promises, breaks promises, takes our money, spends our money. I say term limits. Maybe the first U.S. gov'ment had some honest folks. We don't have anyone like Washington or Adams now."

"So the government can be corrupt and get away with screwing us?"

"I'm sayin' we gotta term limit the Congress. They can't make a lot of money in gov'ment if they are gone in two, four, or six years. And, we the people, gotta stop buying the shit from the asshole liars. We don't care if they lie to us. If we started carin', they'd stop lying or they'd never git to D.C. or they'd shape up."

Shake took a pull on his cup and got back to his point.

"MLK didn't want the gov'ment to give black folks money or pass laws so we could get special treatment. King wanted the gov'ment to make sure black folks had the same opportunity as white folks. Don't treat me no different, good or bad.

Treat me like you would treat a white person. If I do a good job, pay me. If I commit a crime, throw my ass in jail. Don't treat me no different. And black folks gotta stop acting different which gets me back to my answer. We gotta stop teaching 'different.'

Affirmative action is bullshit. Just unlock the doors, unlock the gates, and take off the roof. Don't give me no damn step stool or ladder. Gov'ment gotta stop 'helpin' me. We are a long way from MLK but you wouldn't know it with folks like Farrakan thumpin the box. Let me break it down. You a Cowboy fan?"

"No."

"What the hell's wrong with you?"

Shake belly laughed and Mark felt it on his own stomach.

"Do you watch Football? Do you know the players?

"Yeah, sure."

"Okay, Listen ta me. Troy Aikmen is a damn good quarterback. Emmit Smith is a damn good running back. Michael Irvin has got the hands and the wheels, know what I'm sayin? My man Troy is white. Emmit and Michael are brothers. Now, here comes some affirmative action dumbass, wanna put Emmit behind the snap and get Troy running all over the damn field.

Or they wanna put Michael at QB and tell Emmit to coach the damn team. You folla? They don't care if Troy can't run worth a shit. I mean, he's good enough out of the pocket but he's no damn running back.

The affirmative action dumbass tells the league, 'We need more black coaches and we need more black quarterbacks.' Wreck the damn team with that shit. I ain't sayin' no blacks should coach or QB. I'm sayin', shut the fuck up and let every man do what they good at.

If someone doesn't hire a black man because he's black, then that's they loss, if the black man has something to offa. That coach back in Jackie's day, that Dodger coach or owner, Ricky something. He saw that Jackie Robinson was the man and he got him on. Why? Because Jackie had it and Jackie brought it. Affirmative action says you get the job even if you don't have it or don't bring it and that's fucked up.

Cowboys are going to go to the Super Bowl and they'll win the damn thing because everybody is doing what they do best. Who cares about the damn wrapping? Stop talking about the damn wrapper. I'll let you get back to Rush. You okay, Mark, for white guy."

Shake smiled and extended his hand. Mark took it.

"Where'd you get the nickname Shake?"

"Because when I walk, the ground shakes. I used to play ball."

Shake got up and it was as if he had blocked the sun as he stood over Mark. "I'll see you around." As he passed, Mark could feel tiny tremors under his own soles. Mark turned Limbaugh back on.

"...Wait a minute! Don't listen to some white cracker named Johnny..."

Limbaugh was running a Paul Shanklin bit. Mark looked down the street at Shake. The man was a natural giant. He could have been blocks away and Mark would still be able to recognize the Man. ~

Strange to wake up and find

that it's still today.

Same clothes, no rose,

same purchase price on display.

A time contender pretending to win

more precious ground.

By sleep and dream which make my toss and loss

more profound.

Odd to sit up and feel the glowing fade of the sun,

when one last drink was one too many, my loneliness

overrun.

Then thoughts from phone calls,

As I turn down the bed.

Dread nightly calm, the sheets

embalmed with what was spoken,

what was said.

The second sleep comes

with the help of a prayer

and a friend. The exile looks

for the familiar and the foreign

to share hands.

But the wind is different, and

it blows the vanes to insane claims

of direction.

And you're not here, my only means

of affection.

Clocks and sun dials are keepers

not makers of time.

Watchmen and guardians,

Faceless, part-time, ticketeers

for the terrestrials. Counting breaths,

marking deaths, dance ephemeral to music

eternal, just above the floor. And I watch

with them the end of day into night

without sight of tomorrow or the next.

There is no context for pretext

for hope to conjure more than sorrow:

 a way, a breath, and a thought. ~

The high-up windows

allow light not air, no sight

but despair of what lives

outside these walls.

The high ceiling turns down

the reach, the touch. Not even

a ladder or stacked tables would

bring a tall man close. "I rub my face

to remember yours." Pinch the skin

to remember.

Rows and columns of us,

piles and planks.

Nothing in the pocket,

nothing up the sleeve.

The shoes I walked

in old San Francisco made

the suit and the watch chain

reasonable, the vest and tie

essential, the hat—a given,

given the time.

I made for the docks.

The bustle of commerce concealed me.

But I slipped on a fish right in front of

the blue and black,

flat on my back, like a crab

 off the block,

helpless, a few feet

from open water.

The walls and windows

are made for resident guests.

The songs are meant to get away

up and through the vents

to the birds. The words are

the only ones to escape. They

get us as far as the roof.~

Something to write on

Some place to stay

For words to become memory

or scenes in a play.

Someone to cry on

Someone not here

Transcending the moment

translating the beer.

I made it plain when I left you

that I would return. You made it

clear that you were surely uncertain.

A drive down to somewhere, a place

setting for one. A parking lot, a yard sale,

a carnival campout, a revival of the ghosts

and guests I met while not listening to you.

Cheap conversation in a robe on the street.

Tin cup or can, holy man barefeet.

He shouts in his mind and his thoughts

crash up against tight teeth, prayers beneath

the skin, heartbeat below his chin.

Brushing the pads in a one-foot waltz,

the climb up the mountain away from

the snow is a fool who believed the greener glass

in which the alchemist bottles depression.

Pretension shows the heart,

pretending spends the mind.

Is truth only a fan when you're

neck-high in gravel

popping the gavel

too close, to bury

what we were suppose

to be? ~

Jumping from the 1st story

shows lack of commitment.

Drinking half the bottle means

you only wanted a ride.

Toeing a sidewalk tightrope or

skimming a bullet, just not

strictly strychnine, not the

long wrist peel.

The dead-serious are quiet.

Their drama is beneath others,

backstage, behind the rack lights,

in front of you.

Death isn't crowded but

first and only you.

Funerals shroud the living

in a drop of what you drank daily.

Hindsight and playback are

reflection and echo.

You beat the curve.

You had the one extra nerve

to trust oblivion.

Why didn't someone

waist-rope down to your

bedside before you

drank the rest,

took the rest, before you

completed the line?

Why didn't you "why" while you were here?

Why didn't anyone ask?

Is that why you waited,

for someone to ask? ~

A feeling unrelated

and scene out of view,

with actors I imagine,

the composites of dramatic residue.

I am in their ranks,

among the upright in the hard collars,

men planning to act, men as heroes

before the breach. Only a pause, a lull, a doze,

and I'm back with the women talking about

their children. I suppose

it's natural for them. And normal

for me to want sleep. ~

<u>The Longer Life</u>

Women live longer than men

...because of fear.

A weaker creature's survival instincts

are acute and defined for safety and security.

Men are stronger and this truth, if misinterpreted,

promotes pride, delusion, and recklessness.

Attraction to difference brings men and women together. Admiration for the other, the edition of, and addition to something impossible alone, but I digress.

Women are cleaner than men. They want power and control over threats to their security and safety therefore any germ, piece of dirt, or trash, however small, must be eradicated. Do women live longer because they pay more attention to danger and are prepared for every contingency? I believe one way to understand the longevity of women is consider "the purse."

I am not talking about money or income, but the bag with the strap that most women carry about everywhere until they get to their place of living which is one big purse holding all their necessities and wants. It explains why little by little all my things are being thrown out or relegated to the garage. A woman keeps what will ensure her survival.

Why purses? Men try to have purses but the comedy writes itself and men are left to settle for pockets and wads. We have briefcases, attachés, backpacks, knapsacks, fanny packs, and satchels.

Backpacks are practical for the young but hardly useful for the day-to-day working man. Fanny packs look silly and don't hold enough. I thought that a tool belt might work for most guys on the job. But it doesn't really go with a two-piece suit and that's my point.

Women can pull off the purse-look. There is a purse for every walk of life and no one laughs at them except other women which prompts the offended party to go out and buy a different purse hence, the need for more than one in the armory.

The purse is the woman's tool belt. It's a bit of home. It's a home away from home. Maybe it identifies an aspect of the nature of women. One thing women can say almost universally is that their bodies are designed to hold, carry, and protect another human being. Women are purses. Hmm..., they are divine handbags...No, this isn't sounding right. Okay, let's just stick with the first part. Women live longer than men. And by golly, they deserve to. ~

Driving through LA on 210W

arguing with Siri about the

existential nature of I-5 north,

Highway 5, Interstate 5, the big

long thing with the red, white, and

blue signs all up and down it, damn it!~

The color of promise

is the relief of a rainbow

after the death of all mankind

in water.

The renewal of hope,

the life I wanted is in

front of me, and not

in the past.

Eyes forward

butt in back,

vision for the possible

and the smell behind me.

The windstorm woman

blew over me and changed

the lay of my land. All my

buildings for the last five months

thrown in a tumble,

jumbling my dream

of a managed life. It didn't

take much from her: words in

a final tone, forced me

down the 5,

and away from the small city.

The weather followed me,

her decision in gusts. I packed

quickly for the sudden change

and the untimely departure.

Would a sailor or a seaman

make a better husband? Do

they fare better leaving the

weather at home to face the

unpredictable certainties and

rages of foul seasons on the ocean?

No, not an island but

inland from the peninsula, a point

accessible from the main. More men would

live underground if not for the sun and life.

More women would dig, if they were so earthed.

I sit on wet blue prints, with red fingers,

and white grays holding black ropes to

boats in port.

To leave the shore, I must

describe the shore, pay

attention to its shape,

its function. To understand

that it cannot leave you.

To get here, we must travel,

coming in from...

The docks are designated but

the beach is not an official end, but a

pause between lands.

I sit insignificant before

the greatness of the other sea. ~

God's Sanction Against Time Travel

I

Because no one would want to be here now.

All ships to what would be "the right moment",

the right time for the love note to her desk four

over and one up.

The time just before curtain,

to correct the word or mood,

or not go on at all.

To another town where you could

be the new kid again and again and never

grow old or tired of hearing

the first hello for the thousandth time.

II

We are stopped from going back

because we all need "we all" here now.

God gave us imagination for travel: to write,

draw, paint, sing, and play away

from "now."

Away from teeth and cuts,

an eye cast near, over, or

her looking pretty

-distant.

We can't go back to

tying the strings more quickly,

and the bows in a row to show

prodigious empathy.

We cannot return to the first dance

and change the song, the partner, the

room or church, or park or dark light

foundation, when the night was useless

to withstand a chance meeting.

Death pretends a dramatic random but

wise ones pull out the racks to cool the pies

and set the clocks without candlelight.

III

We cannot go back to simpler.

We will find it again, at the end,

when the lesson has been fully

learned.

Never taught,

Never learned,

if we go back.

Never begun.

Consequences wait forever

for their cue.

Imperfect birth to fallen faller

falling forward,

facing what all

attempt,

while they love.

IV

If we could go back in time,

no one would be left here/now

but the wise and those too tired to

make the trip.

What would the streets and shops

reveal if we all went to what we

thought was our point of ascension?

And would those who built the "around

us" erase the "around us" because they

traveled back and changed their minds

about the "around us" they made. So much

of everyone's past makes up our present.

V

The wise and the old

regret and do not. Back there

in youth, capturing, grasping

to grow up, rocking-chair rocketing back

for the prom and "yes"!,

instead of the parking-lot vomit

with your best man to be.

VI

The long wide hall

starts short and narrow then

widens as we dream and

fool about

for meaning.

The last 20 or 30 years sharpens

and dulls the edges and corners of

a door, wide enough for one.

      We slow our steps and stretch the time

between nights to make windows and

flower boxes, distracting us from the only

time travel we are allowed.

God will not let us go back

and double our sins.

We are given our limited skin.

And after our brief time here,

we will be released from flesh

and time will be dead forever.~

Playing Politics

Within the last two years, I've heard the term "identity politics." I crafted a definition for politics myself about 15 years ago. I played it off a few people and got

no genuine affirmation that I was onto something.

Rush Limbaugh started using the term but used it only to describe a specific aspect of politics. Identity politics, roughly, is identifying one's self by belonging to a group, either by birth or by choice. Some women identify themselves as feminists, victims of various injustices identify with those who were also ill-treated. I would like to go out on a limb here with the distinct possibility of being wrong.

When I think of the word "politics," two concepts come to mind. In the 1960's, on TV and in movies, I heard phrases like, "My husband is thinking of "going into politics." It was another way of saying that a person was "running for office." Politics then was an umbrella term or category of employment of the politician.

Looking at a politician the way one would look at an electrician, it is easy to understand the job he or she would be tasked to do. Electricians work with electricity. Politicians make and execute policy.

Enter the phrase "playing politics" and we move away from the honorable to what most politicians are known for now. What is "playing politics?" What does one do to earn such an accusation?

Here is my definition. See if this is a partial, local, or universal truth. Before I define, let me make it clear that I am not talking about the politician or policy maker.

"All politics is the manipulation of identity."

I took my little definition and plugged it into a few recent situations. When a office-holder lies about his own record to appear to his voters in a better light, he is "playing politics," manipulating his own identity, in other words, lying. When a candidate distorts his opponents words, record, positions, he is manipulating the identity of the other.

The manipulations are always lies: deception, misrepresentation, mischaracterization, distortions, and omissions. Any form of lie or falsehood intended to

manipulate one's own worth, value, uniqueness, glory---
identity, is politics. We have gotten away from a
politician proud to identify himself as a politician in the
classic sense.

The goal of politics is power. A few simple
questions to ask ourselves about our current crop of
elected officials are, "Why do they want the job?" and
"Are they honest?" Now before you accuse me of living
in Rainbowland, let me push back.

We have accepted for so long now that politicians
lie, that they make promises they probably won't keep.
We, or the media anticipates, an "October surprise"
every presidential election. What is an October surprise
but a piece of information, an action, a tape, a recording,
a video that will manipulate the identity of the target.

What is true about the October Surprise is that it
is always negative. It is usually known weeks and
months before it is used. It can be true and it is a bonus
if the ratio between the truth and the lie is tipped
toward credibility.

What is the complaint of the electorate and the
minority of civic-minded individuals when the debates
and the primary season are upon us. It is Entertainment
vs. Issues. It is the Policy maker vs. the Politician. Policy
is the actual job up for grabs. But policy is boring. A

brilliant economist, accountant, or an administrator is no match for the politician playing politics.

Trump is an anomaly because he was an entertaining non-political private sector businessman who played politics and manipulated the identity of everyone around him and could not himself be redefined by his opponents. He did not play by the established rules laid down by the lying politicians. He was overt in his lies, visible, not subtle.

What is the antidote for "playing politics" or lying in all forms? The remedy is truth. We need the truth in all its forms and applications and we need laws of accountability for those in office and for those seeking office. There should be laws and penalties for media who propagate lies, deceptions, or distortions in favor of one candidate over the other. Harry Reid lied about Mitt Romney not paying his taxes. Reid has not faced any consequences for this blatant lie he told during a presidential campaign.

Candidates should be penalized for any lie or mischaracterization they promote during a campaign. They should also be penalized if they lie about their own record of achievement.

If we look at each candidate as someone who is interviewing for a job, which they are, then shouldn't

we, as their potential employer, ask that they answer
our questions honestly and that their resumes are
factual? We would also not hire someone who
besmirches with lies those who are competing for the
same job. We have accepted this culture of falsehood for
too long. We need to be able to look at a person's
truthful record of accomplishment, listen to their ideas,
hear them address the issues, and not have some
"interpreter" manipulating the information.

Is it possible for honest men and women to speak
and be heard when they choose to run to serve the
public as a leader, as a policy maker? If a politician is a
liar and corrupt, evidence should be reported and they
should be labeled as such.

There should not be an acceptable level of lying
and deceit. If we could, as voters, not look for the
entertainer, and if the media outlets could stop
contexting our candidates in "fight of the century" terms,
maybe we can pick a bunch of capable, boring people
who will really understand what they are doing when
they get to Washington, D.C. ~

Walmart Waltz

Staring down a Walmart aisle,

standing next to the heat-lamp

rotisseries, I reach into a strange

woman's eyes and blink less at the

amputee by the cheese. I am not them

but I am here. I am not them but

wear skin, buy bargain bread, and

holiday flowers.

Fluorescent row-racks above the produce.

Fat people lying to themselves over the lettuce.

The one, thin queen is pierced and tattooed. I would

say, "be still my beating heart" but remember that

I need to renew my blood pressure prescription and

so refrain from the cliché and love. ~

Of Science

"God rejoices at our observations,

is hopeful at our speculations,

 and disappointed in our conclusions."

This attempt at wisdom is flawed by human limitation. God does delight but I'm not sure He rejoices. And does God hope as we do? He is at the beginning, middle, and end of everything. How can He be hopeful, optimistic, or surprised? Therefore, He cannot be disappointed. He has already been present in our future moments of failure. God is love so what does it matter?

We must learn about God from God and not mistakenly create Him in our image. ~

Stop Lying You Stupid, Stupid Woman

I am inspired by politicians

to make such outbursts.

But my faith and belief in God restrain me

from publicly declaring my disdain

for some elected officials.

It is unkind to call someone names.

It is not love.

We strive for civility. We engage

in civil discourse. We try to uphold

decorum. But there is trouble on

the dance floor. The politician prances
to a different tune and steps on our
feet purposefully and provocatively.
Sometimes, due to intellectual
limitations, they act unintentionally
and without malice. Senators and
Congress-men and women
have parliamentary rules and procedures
to play nice. This makes them terrible
as spokespersons for those of us who
are tired of the lies, tired of the manipulation,
tired of our judgment being insulted by
individuals who are only slightly more
intelligent than we are and definitively
more corrupt.

I think President Trump was elected partly
because he was uncivil and rude, speaking truth
to power, saying what the average American
was thinking and feeling. Trump was a release,
an unplanned, anti-establishment apolitical

loudmouth with nothing to lose in the political
world because he never belonged to it.

I was and am still angry and disappointed that
President Trump disparaged and discredited honorable
men and women in the primaries. I was not displeased
when he concentrated his blunt force bravado on the
candidate from the opposing party.

Will Trump redefine political discourse and
civility? Has he already adjusted the bar? In our
attempts in the past to temper our temper with language
fraught with euphemism, we little by little have
removed the sharpness of our rhetoric and its power to
cut through the lies, deception, and propaganda
pumped through our screens by a compromised media.

I wish today's interviewer or reporter would
follow up on statements made by officials in our
government and identify and label the statements as
actual lies, using the word "lie" when reporting. No
more of this--- "...Less than truthful", "...not
forthcoming", or "could not verify..."

Politicians count on our decency to stop us from
holding them accountable. Trump was indecent and it is
quite possible that he was the only one in the
Republican field capable of defeating Hillary Clinton

because of his unwillingness to follow established "political" decorum.

Trump has presented a conundrum to the Christian who believes he or she should be involved in earthly authority and its corresponding politics. We want to live in a moral, ethical, and civil society. We want our elected officials to be moral. Nice guys don't finish at all and the "children of this world are wiser in dealing with their own kind then the children of light." Trump isn't by many measures a fundamentalist Christian. If he was Christ-like, it is conceivable that he would have never entered the political arena, never engaged in the primaries, and never would have gone after Hillary so mercilessly.

I am glad Mrs. Clinton isn't president. I am hopeful that President Trump will take the right steps to bring America closer to its Constitutional design. Far too many Republicans still operate under the wrong impression that government should be involved in extra-constitutional activities. Private citizen Trump, now public servant, just might break this interventionist, big government meddlesome mentality. ~

Easter 2017 (photographed)

The grey valley in the overcast

was my Easter and the eye looking down

on us before blending into heavy air.

My life is different now with you

under this

chasing doom.

We are at the beginning of the last and

this park of trees and geese and red-wings

soothe our fears as we walk together

alone,

never to ask again what we were

meant to be,

but in consent to the present path,

we trust the walk will end well.~

On the edge of leaving again.

On the cusp of returning.

The intent to stay and

the will to find you.

The city distracts and deludes.

The country deprives and hones

me.

Dry grains and herbs in quiet

not the night light open window cafes

and the cover charge for atmosphere,

baked into the flake, pressed into the demi.

Turning from the stage to street level,

where the tall and the beautiful disguise my

presence. Blended common coffee pudge,

the Giamatti mournful eyes aware of shared gravity

depressed for lack of lift, the thoughts of old vexations,

muscle passed present temptations resulting in a smurk.

You know you've met wisdom, if your vision is

sadness and your resolution is love: To see the vanity of
life and reduce its complexities to serving the will of
others. ~

I look tall in the long mirror

hanging on the door and to

my wife when she's not mad

at me.~

When you're a roving substitute teacher,

you're always the new kid on the block and

no one sits with you at lunchtime. That's when

Montague realized that he was better than everyone

else in the staff lounge. He took his brown bag and

his new philosophy out on to the campus and into

the world knowing that the illusion wouldn't last the

day.~

The stories come easy

from the old. A smile opens

the life they remember, those

whom they loved and still love.

The pace of the telling

holds the patience few

who listen for

a hint of themselves. ~

Hanging pictures on the wall

of places

you'll never go.

Driving over bridges

where the waters

used to be

The clothes in the closet

wait for their owner

to be inspired.

A basket overflowing with

plastic fruit, belies the cornicopic

illusion.

Statues are trophies

and people pace around

them, forgetting the feeling

of conquest.

If he could remember

that he lived here, then

he could sleep with his

eyes closed and the guards

could go home.~

"The horse done told me so,"

said the chicken with a tear.

The pig is on the lamb,

trying to find some beer.

The sheep are in a huddle.

Their plan's a little risky.

Blind Bill will go out for a pass

while Wool Willie jacks the whisky.

It's a song I have to sing cuz she's gone.

It's a tune I have to play.

All the animals are drinking in the barn

waiting for me to say:

"It's all yer fault she left. Who wants to

live with a bunch of talking, alcoholic farm animals?

Where's my gun?!" ~

You'll know the end of western civilization is near when
you hear the phrase,

"...to fulfill all your television needs."~

Other books by MJ MONTY

Vox Noir, A Radio Drama (novel---676 pages)

Public Private Places (poetry and humor---123 pages)

ill-Timed Quixotic (poetry from 1980-1998.---154 pages)